Poems From a Wanderer

Philip Lester

Cover Illustration by the author:
A view of Loch Druidibeag, RSPB Nature Reserve, South Uist.

Print ISBN: 978-1-8380177-6-7

These poems are dedicated solely

to the memory of all the brave men

and women of the armed forces

who have given their lives in sacrifice

that we might enjoy our freedom.

Philip Lester

CONTENTS

Philip Lester

The poems in this collection are in reflection of God's creations. Flowers, trees, butterflies, mammals and birds mingled with personal experiences about life and observances of daily experience that often we all have. There is no individual commentary on each poem as it is hoped that each piece will speak for itself. It is the poet's dear wish that this collection will please and remind the reader that God in His infinite wisdom has created all these things for us to treasure and enjoy, and that to Him only should any and all praise be given.

Philip Lester

Lines on the Death of a Mouse

I am sad for thee o mouse,
But the tenants of this house
Objected strong to your presence here.
And on that presence,
Became annoyed in essence
Then baited their ingenious gear.

O believe me 'twas sad
And for me was quite bad
When I heard the trap had sprung.
Some cried their elate
Or some similar state
But I saw now a life was unsung.

They saw not your right,
To feast in delight
Upon breadcrumbs left wasting all day.
Nor greater the heart
That tender, did start
Whose beating they took full away!

Nor saw they dead eyes,
That stared in surprise
Or the visible cause of your hurt,
For them was relief
On catching a thief
And the end to that minuscule dirt.

By a pipit's nest

Down a grassy tunnel once I gentle peeped
And visioned wonder there did I see;
For 'neath those grasses soft and fragile heaped
Six tiny voices called so innocently.

From raised heads, whose eyes were tender blind
Came forth a plea from out that mossy nest,
And voiced as one unto my mind
They called to me, their quiet unseen guest.

Lo! It seemed a plea for all to enter there,
To give thus food to naked ones so small;
Hence show example from a heart of care
No matter who the giver in that grassy hall.

O 'twas such a plea! That spake a need to live
That from each breast did feeling break,
'Twas no wonder that my heart did give
Henceforth a feeling loud that said 'Awake!'

Yet such we miss, for man is often blind -
Much more than pipits naked in the flowery grass.
That sometimes rare we seem to loving find,
Whilst love and joy he seems content to pass.

P. L

The meadow Pipit

Seeing a fox's head mounted on a wall

'Tis a wonder to me how such a vicious look
Can be achieved by consummate skill, it struck
Me at a glance; and surely (I inward said)
Such a gentle, furred and impressive head
Could never contain such ferocity I see –
Or, may it have been by chance or some degree,
Whereby this noble band of hunting horse
And men with hounds, and yes, of course,
The hunt itself on sight of such as thee,
Discovered in alarm that they had eagerly
In vain sought the wrong creature?
And, as if to try and hide embarrassed feature
Settled for your gentle life instead?
Anon, your life dispatched then homeward sped
These hunters with their charmèd prize.
And meeting those gazing and hungry eyes
Of all that knew of this famous chase,
Then sought to save their real disgrace
By contortion of your natural form.
This being so, they went at further length to warm
Their hearts with even falser thought,
That they had in no doubt caught
Some hideous and repulsive beast –
As if they would know, o sad and pained
deceased!

Philip Lester

The Hare Coursers

Look at them! Confident walking,
Sporting with their bony hounds;
And whilst these dogs are busy stalking,
How foolishness resounds.

Their voices echo clear o'er the lake
In hollowed tones from hollowed minds;
And as each step they further take,
My eye close to them binds.

A hare! The hounds have seen their quarry,
Thence swift to pursue in flight.
They race up then down the grassy corrie,
Within my feeling sight.

I feel for the hare with heart a-beating
As back and forth his plan
Is simple in his mind completing,
To escape both hound and man.

Nigh a minute gone! Speed now is waning
The hounds together have wore him full;
The moment nigh, his strength now draining,
His aching senses lull.

A cry! That pierces soul and air
And echoes deep in mine,
Thence no more runs the hunted hare
With full his broken spine.

The hounds now at their final task,
Their masters' smiles now feature;
And I myself one question ask:
Who is greater, man or creature?

Philip Lester

The Stricken Elm

Had your fellows grown as tall as thee, o elm,
Would not some other have been violent struck
And made to burn in sadness like to thee?
For that lightning bolt full savage took
Thy topmost branches; and the roosting rook
Was driven from thee most hastily,
From attempt to sleep and semi-waking realm.

Now hast thou burned this long April day
The glowing embers by early morning light
Have danced and sparkled full 'til eve;
And proceeding downward have in further blight
Journeyed fire in shimmering embers bright,
Nor doth it want to mercied leave
Thy trunk unburned and crackles in display.

Yet two more days have passed since the storm
Took full away such foliaged tresses
As once were thine; thence half a day besides
Hath seen the labourer visit and full he presses
Home both saw and axe, the rope caresses
The bough and branches that newly died
And astride he steps o'er part that smoulders warm.

Then, commenced he to stack his woody load
With such as can be used upon a fire,
His gnarled hands as old as gnarled wood
Placing firm in heaps the elm; and by the byre
Throughout his hard and daylong hire,
He stacks with thought neither bad nor good
This once great elm, twice killed and aged growed.

The Oak and the Daisy

'How mighty I stand' said the English oak
To the daisy who lay far beneath,
'And all other trees I jealous provoke
From forest to pasture or heath.
My limbs are stout, my strength unique
My foliage exuberantly flows;
The tops of my branches birds eagerly seek,
Their lives I protect from all foes.'

'I have little to recommend me,' the daisy replied,
'Comparable thus to all flowers.
There is little I have,' she wearily sighed,
'For most things over me towers.
I have but a face that is yellow and small
And petals of whiteness around.
Of leaves I have few to upon them soft call
And cover, but not any ground.'

'I see you are small,' the oak spake out loud.
'But acorns your size have I known.
And never have I to greatest winds bowed,
Nor as thee by the slightest wind blown.
I bow not to storm, nor even to time,
For centuries have I in me.
The rain washes from me the slightest of grime
And the sun promotes growth as you see!'

'I cannot compare to thee, for as you say
For size and proportion well shown,
My own little life may last but a day
And then I am almost full grown.'
But the oak answered not to the daisy's remark
For the woodman had chosen his pile.
Lo! The axe had cut deep in the oak's aged bark,
And the daisy she put on a smile.

An Otter Seen from a Headland

Through waters deep and gentle warm
The otter swam to me.
And 'neath the ocean tide her form,
Swam deep and gracefully.

She laughed at seals upon her way,
She mocked the gulls above;
And joyful in her watered play
She crossed the harboured cove.

By waves that crashed upon the rocks
Toward this headland sound,
The sea's great power she seemed to mock
Her grace the waters crowned.

And 'neath the place where I lay by
She swam and moved and dined,
Then deep I looked within her eye
And wonders did I find.

Of seas unswam and fish to chase
Upon the oceaned head,
Of salmon caught in playful race
And eaten, tail to head.

And all the while a laugh I heard
Within her secret thought.
Beneath her frame so sleek and furred,
Her life I wholly caught.

She laughed for joy in thought complete
That all throughout her days,
The voice of freedom would her greet
In all its countless ways.

A laughing smile thence out of view
She slid beneath the foam,
And crowning tide with bubbles new
She embraced her watery home.

To the Swallow

O such life I see within this bird,
He never seems to cease
From swooping past in vision blurred
With ne'er a stop for peace,
To chattering upon each fenced wire
His calm finds no release.
Twofold families he gently sires
(Nay, not twice but make it three.)
His young raised just as urgently
To race o'er churched spires.

But come September on the fenced place
He sits and bides his time,
And my mind instead begins to race
Upon his life sublime.
And I await his leaving hour
When ends the summered time,
For then his magic seasoned power
Has nigh but run its course,
Whence summer, who is within his source,
Will before the autumn cower.

To a Small Copper Butterfly

Who would have your colours bright
Would choose this beach of grey?
It seems to me your little light
Is vivid as night to day.
And how handsomely upon the kale
You sit in sunlit rays,
And all around upon you, now seems pale
As you alone I praise.

Such wings of burnished gold I see,
Such beauty as you rest.
How happy am I in such company
And well do I feel blessed.
For the beach is lit wher'er you land
And lo! I must confess
That when God saw this drabbish sand
With you He did it dress!

To a Peacock Butterfly

I watched him as he sprightly danced
Upon the summer breeze.
O how gaily mannered he pranced,
Beneath the sunlit trees.

He landed on a scented fern
And opened up his wings
His blaze of colour I did discern
Outside his darklet rings.

Thence circlet orbs like painted eyes
Impressive matched in shade,
Fell back and forth in brief surprise
As on the fern he laid.

Art thou aware of thy lovely sight?
Or how perfect your colours blend?
O living glory, o pure delight,
Rare do I see thee, welcome friend.

'Tis sad thy beauty upon the earth
Lasts brief, but I commend the thought
That lost in part might be thy worth
If sight of thee were often caught.

To the Tormentil

Of all the flowers that nature thoughtful weaves
Upon the face of her wondrous loom,
There is a flower with small and gentle leaves
That doth the moorland grasses oftimes groom,
'Tis yellow tormentil!

And when dawns the heady month of gloried June,
Upon the hillside here I often pensive lie
Thence with harmonious feeling upon my grassy dune
Unto that special flower cast my praisesome eye,
To little Tormentil!

O brightest one, if colours could but sing,
What songs would thence be heard from thee?
What joys would from out thy petals ring
As sorrows from thee would hasty flee,
O golden Tormentil!

To a Bluebell

Simply, thou art a delight, o flower!
And I perceive that nature's power
Has caused your many heads to cower
In delicate bloom;
So that off your painted lips
Each dewdrop gently slips
To quit thee and all grasses groom.

In shyness hangs thy swaying head,
And where the daisies' bloom are wed
Above this grassed and earthy bed,
Ten thousand of you and more!
And o'er the hedged bank
'Neath trees in perfect rank,
Ten times that rise and joyful pour.

I wonder not that nature firmly gave
Great space to thee and further save
Each shaded spot or where you crave,
Yourself to be.
For the rain you keep not back,
With each flowerous sack,
But give most freely to the earth with glee!

Think not, o flower, that in my heart
Another could quite as thee impart
Nor through my feelings so easily chart
Such loving feeling.
O gem of brightest blue,
So wonderful in view,
My heart to thee is always gently stealing!

The Little Robin

Though other birds retreat at will
When winter comes, there is one still
To greet the cold winds loud and shrill,
The little robin.
And though his fellows brave the cold
With shivered look and miseried hold,
There is one still to greet it bold –
The little robin.

Who is it sings whilst others mourn
As if the early winter dawn
Had changed to summer freshly born?
The little robin.
Who is it cheers midwinter's grey?
And greets the snow with breast so gay?
Who heralds Yuletide Christmas Day?
The little robin.

He holds the secret of the frost
And though winds howl and trees are tossed
He alarmeth not, nor counts the cost,
The little robin.
I heard him singing on the bough
When snows before him firm did plow
He minded not the least I trow,
The little robin.

A Goshawk Chased

Beneath a glaring summer sun
I watched a scene unfold,
A goshawk raced and swirled in run
From a raven that did her scold.
She twisted this way, then about
Then reeled about in flight;
And to my mind there seemed no doubt
That she was lost in plight.
But thence the scene in instant changed,
The pursued turned full around;
And all the scene was rearranged
As the moment change was found.
The goshawk struck the raven's brow,
Her talons pierced her prey;
Thence down they went to the vale below
Where firm her meal next lay.
Was she playing all the while?
The thought in me resides.
Did she employ but playful guile?
The question in me bides.

Poems From a Wanderer

P.L

To a Kingfisher

Secret splendour of the brook
With wings of azure blue
I had of thee but a glimpsed look
As up the stream you flew.
No doubt unto your mossy nest
Within some brambled bank,
Where close your mate in feathered breast
Holds darling young in rank.
Or was it else to some shaded spot
'Neath trees that give their shade,
That in you flew to where your cot
Gives rest within some glade?
Where silvered minnows timid gleam
That to thine eye but flash;
And to their presence there 'twould seem
You are some waterous splash.
But thou a halcyon art to me,
More than mere vision blue:
For full thou art of secrecy
And sighted moments, few.

'Halcyon'

To a Goldfinch

I saw thee first but two weeks past
First building in the bough
And to the tree, then bare, I cast
My thoughts to wondering how.
Concealment was in my mind,
Thence, how such a tender brood
That was to thee this spring assigned
Once dam your song had wooed.
Thence feeble thought came into my head,
I said in my mind, no sense
Had caused thee to be fully led
To build in leaves not dense!
Yet later here I ashamed stand
For the full leafed tree I find,
And perfect concealed is the nest you planned;
Thou seest! 'Tis I who is blind!

The Goldfinch

The Night Visitors

Deep beneath my feet in a mossy cavern
Half slumbrous nigh to dusk
The badger in his hollow tavern
Stirs on his bed of musk.
Then softly calls, a need to stir
Now day has safely fled,
And movement through his soilèd fur
Proceeds, from tail to head.

And slow, up for night is calling,
He wakes full and lumbers to
The settled mouth and soiled walling
Where waits the moon in view.
Then once having tasted of the air,
He moves that all is well,
And to the nightly woodland stair
Sets off into the dell.

Thence, close behind his leaving frame
Another striped head inclined
Now shakes herself and calls by name
Her three young cubs behind.
And off they go, behind the brook
The sow and offspring queue,
Like some proud shepherd with a flock
To pastures old and new.

A Lakeland Eagle Seen

Who but the raven alone would dare
To drive from out his rocky lair
The eagle's might, and cause with beated wings
To seek some peace upon the summered air?
Thence, determined he almost silent brings
His life to seek the skies so free and fair.

Thence up! O'er craggy pinnacles below
He climbs swift up, and doth higher show
Such grace and power in his wakened flight,
As onward firm his gliding form doth go
Mid sunshine cloud and dewy morning bright
Whilst will to roam doth in him passioned flow.

And now, yet rising higher o'er the rivered dale,
His imagery small begins to slowly fail,
As 'neath a cloud he gathers by and by
Pursuing flight within a cerulean veil.
Moved on by purpose, emitting out his cry
And to the Lord of life gives voice and loudest hail.

Nightfall in Kentmere

The sun bids farewell to the day now spent
O'er the hills above the vale of River Kent
And the lamb calls plaintive in the evening air
To his mother, who feeds on the hillside stair.
But all else is hushed now as shadows fall
And the warbler sends out his last sweet call.
Thence the cuckoo distant makes his presence felt
As shapes into darkness begin to melt.
Lo! The first rabbit emerges to begin his play,
Where grassy blades about his form now sway.
And the sound of sheep upon their grassy quest
Lull soft the mind to thoughts of welcome rest.
Now the badger emerges from his earthy sett
Thence scents the air yet feels regret;
Delighting not in shadows on the scene,
And returns to where his daylong sleep has been.
Thence a tawnied owl calls from wholesome breast
And bids a hail to the darkening west,
Now off his bough with bright eye keen
Flies roving to see what his hunger might glean.
Now every flower fast have closed their buds,
Along hillside bare and late benighted woods;
And small creatures move upon the grassy floor
Eagerly busied to this nighttime lure.
Lo! The bat flitting over the farmyard place
Her form from insect to moth doth race,
But darkened formed against the failing light
In silhouette vivid against the fall of night.

Thence we reach the farmyard gate,
And raise the latch in this eventide late.
We bid adieu and then thoughts of sleep
Are crowned with final calls of sheep,
For far across the vale are returned in sound
The voices of other ewes on higher ground,
Who pace the quiet of this peaceful fall
Of night and final curlew's call.
Thence down the lane and to our home,
We close another page of our lifelong tome,
And drift with thoughts of earned sleep
To await the sun who o'er the hills will creep,
With blessed rays to chase the night away
And strike with gold this curtain fall of grey.

A Long-tailed Tit Nest Destroyed

How long they laboured to build this home
Of lichen, moss, cobweb and feather;
And thence I watched them happy comb
Each natured fabric to halt all weather.
Retiring oft to line complete within
Such builded perfection gathered from nought.
A softness where eggs but wafer-thin
Might safe be laid; and from this brought
Forth a beauty more into this needful world
Of harsh reality, doubt and sin.

Yet beauty I perceive is not felt by all,
And oft 'neath the mischief's hands she struggles brief;
Hence when an ignorance doth oftimes fall,
She waits in hope; but oftimes some thief
Will seize upon his vain illicit prize,
And foolishness blinds him to the truth.
Thence in his heart then firmest lies
The weight of folly called ignorant youth.

For oft, some child into a warm and perfect nest
Hath thrust his hand to meet some miracle there,
And to unfeeling and inhuman breast
Clasped close an egg, his mind devoid of care.
Thence wandered off to glade or grassy seat
And none the wiser to some life now lost,
Yet even more the pain of loss complete
As grieving parents count their painful cost.

Long Tailed Tit

Watching migrating birds at Galtabacks, Sweden

Upon a shoreline in a cold grey dawn, patiently waiting,
A southerly breeze now blowing o'er the land.
Thence warmth! The sun, fiery hued
Thence creeping slow o'er the frost-bit trees,
Eager to pronounce a glory.
Thence life! All stirring woken by her rising
And to the sounds above I happy listening move,
To the hundred wearied travellers overhead,
Those gentle souls with small hearts beating!
And by and by a hundred more their kind follow
Ever moving, ever onward to avoid old winter's grip.
Thence others pass, smaller formed in groups
Lit by a common purpose in varied callings,
Voicing life in the cold morning air,
Impressed by nature's warning, joyful sounding;
O how great their courage in hearts so tender!

To the Cherry Tree

O what is there but to compare
To the cherry tree in flower?
All else in sight seems naught so fair
Before her blossomed power.
See how her dress hath fullness showed
Each petal soft and growed,
As shamelessly she throws her gown
With beauty firm bestowed.

So soft she looks as if each wind
Could melt each gentle bloom,
And how easy doth the mind then find
A worthy praising room.
Her gentlest pinks, her radiant whites
Are soft in which the eye delights.
O how lovely now the air she crowns
With all her blossomed flights!

Upon a Country Lane

There is something about a country lane
That lifts the down-pressed heart,
A certain something that I fain
Would have right from the start.

To walk beside these hedged worlds
Where nature's secret thought
Lies hidden and yet, as scene unfurls,
The whole of it is caught.

Where spiders about their devious task
A-building their pearled lines,
Join butterflies with their wings enmasked
Upon some flower-graced spines.

Where whiskered faces might appear
From out the hedged aisles,
And quite as swiftly may sudden veer
Into the grassborne piles.

I would not change the sight of this
Nor a chance to walk again
Beneath each shaded tree that twist
Their arms above the lane.

To hear the dunnock in his bower,
Enchanting in his song,
Is as to me as a precious flower
Whose memory lingers long.

Unhappy kings and queens must reign
Within each royal home,
But I upon my countried lane
My empires happy roam.

If wrens were not so hasty
and vocal they would be
overlooked

The Jackdaw

He struts about upon the lawn
His eye a-piercing wide,
And keen he walks divided torn
'Mid scavenging and pride.

He seizes firmly in his beak
(that dark and sombre tool)
Each edible morsel he did seek
With eyes of greyish jewel.

He weighs me strangely with an eye
And cautious walks away,
In backward glance I see him spy
To where his path once lay.

He chases off the fledgling small
And steals from all around,
The broken bread thrown down to all
Upon the verdant ground.

He lands upon the garden wall
Regardful not of one,
And looking all about he calls
Then climbs into the sun.

How proud ye are o jackdaw bird,
Yet proud I would not be,
If I had thy nature or voice so heard,
Contained alike to thee!

To a Willow Warbler

Sweet voice of summer, the glade is thine!
By night of conquest and by song so fine
That pours throughout this bower.
O list! How beneath thy beautied voice
All other songbirds scarce rejoice,
Ashamed voiced beneath thy power!

The robin sings almost as well
From out the green and lonely dell;
The wren in force of song bursts forth,
And blackbird sends his joyous sound
Where the bramble bank is wound,
Yet they are not thy worth.

But teach them thus to sing as sweet
And no longer will they then retreat
When sweet song proceeds from thee.
Give forth thyself in delicate art
From out thy full and melodious heart
Thence shall they listen, not flee.

Yet, I sense a purpose in your song,
That liquid resonance sweet and long,
Which proceeds from out thy breast;
A sense of memory that long repeats
As if a teacher to his pupilled seats
Hath in teaching his song addressed.

Philip Lester

By Brotherswater in September

'Tis September! The blackberries lustre black
Like dull jewels amid the sparse hedgerow,
Yet here and there some fragile flower
Peeps still timid from out the grassy bank,
Giving forth a full yet fading glory
Before winter chills overcome their splendour.
But lo! I look from hence to autumned hills
And though they look seeming changeless
Steeped in rich and distant grasses,
See thou close! For in nearer view the grass
Hath also begun to lose a richness once again,
And soon a gaunt and greyish look will appear
To meet each full and questing eye.
Yet I cannot long observe things distant,
But seem needful of objects near
And hence to fields again my eye I cast.
I watched the lambs for a time,
Those self-same ones who came in March.
O, how woefully they gaze and warily now
Upon their changing world, their coats now drab
No longer golden, but more like their dams
Who feed afar, no longer caring for their forms.
Thence up the lane I wander 'mid silent hush.
No longer doth the blackbird or chaffinch sing
As they did in their joy-filled summertime,
But the robin alone or some vibrant wren
Bursts forth occasional from a nearby copse;
Whilst overhead the late martin in thought
Of distant Afric feeds final before his journey.
But I love this time of year!

When fields are newly readied and the promise
Of things new to arrive invade my mind;
The gentle calm of vales now in full.
'Tis a time as it were when God in His wisdom
Waits patient before His new-created canvas
With brush poised in hand to paint the scene.
And one, knowing the work of the great artist
Can only wait in anticipation and awe
Of growing colours yet still to come,
Falling marvellous before each mortal eye;
As each and every vale and lane expectantly
And eagerly awaits this true artist's visit.

P. L

Composed by the window of 'Browfoot'

From out this window as I peaceful sit
Fairfields screes are brightly lit
With snows that glint 'neath a wondrous sun
(whose work by eve seems scarce begun)
To warm the scattered snowy caps,
That round her like a mantle wraps
Through mists that round her run.
And there, close by this warming house
A pair of circling buzzards now rouse
The air with their mewing cries;
And thence with aerial manoeuvre hies
The eye to follow their progressed flight
Each wing reflective of sunborne light,
As o'er the meadow they joyful rise.
Such framed scenes encaptured clear
Through windows bring the mountains near
As if they could almost be held.
The buzzards, who for a moment dwelled
In the January sky, touched brief by the soul
Each wind-borne leaf
Into the mind began to meld;
The sheep grazing on the lea
By the dry stone wall could a picture be
As a canvas upon a galleried wall.

Nothing moves now. The plaintive call
Of the buzzard gone, its author also from the scene.
The ewes are stilled on the fields of green,
Their minds engrossed, permanent feeding fall
To the flowerless and wintered grass.
The rainy showers begin to firmly pass
In gentlest fashion upon the village lane.
But now sudden in strength resolute begins to gain
A hold upon the scene outside.
Yet, in me still, the previous scene doth bide,
Forever pleasant through each memoried vein
Despite the fall of thee, o blessed rain.

By Derwentwater

Near where waters tumble over stones, I sit
And almost in speech, conversing soft is writ
Such melodious tones of harmony.
Lo! From off the bridge where once the drover
His teamed belongings by horse once pulled
And regular up this scenic path was seen,
This country lover!
With labouring horse in rhythmic nodding lulled,
Encouraged on in step by gypsy rover.

Here too the passage full of market sheep was told
The shepherd with attendant dog, full dolled
Out in existence in a hireling manner.
And here, upon such summery days as heated fall
May he quiet have stood in reverent thought
And to his faithful in recollect,
Made short a call.
Encouraging too with wooden crook in action wrought
Upon sheep who chose to stray beside the bridged wall.

Derwentwater, thy mirrored glass before me lies!
And thy historied isles in bounded vision lie
To full pronounce thy beautied fall,
Fair reminiscent of Como's imagined scene,
And dominated by thee, o Skiddaw!
What genial sight and impressive show
Is seen from this arbour green,
And how this vale doth full her radiance pour
Her richest hues complete on landscaped mien.

Let others have their favoured rustic spot,
Some personal delight from off some grassy cot.
For me, o lake with all your tree filled isles
As thee St. Herbert, penned well by local bard
And thee Lord's Isle, once the seat of earls.
There you all lie in this sequestered place,
Full glacial scarred,
Whilst all about the mountained circlet curls
And in heaven's vault, each cloud is playful jarred.

In Dorothy's Grove

I found a hardy stone one eve
Which firm upon it said
That oftimes past where path did weave
A maid once was frequent led.
And to this place within the wood
The lass was wont to stray,
Thence happy in a reveried mood
Dwell out her summered day.

And I wondered then what caused the lass
To sit within this place,
For hour on hour happy pass
Ere sometimes gently pace.
And so I sat and closed my eyes,
Thence visioned in my mind
Whatsoever of heaven or earthly ties
Once here did gentle bind.

I visioned her walking by the fold,
Her shawl wrapt loose around;
A slender tome in her hand did hold
As she moved with scarce a sound.
Her sombre bonnet with fallen bow
Was gathered 'neath her face,
That spoke a gentleness, oh how
She moved within this place.

Then up the path she made her way
The pastoral woodland maid,
Whilst all about the summered day
In sun and shadow played.
And 'neath a tree in blessed shade
She placed her woollen shawl,
As all before her heart was weighed
Each blessing, great and small.

'Twas then I realised why she chose
This rugged woodland path,
Where sweetest grass still tender grows
Within her aftermath.
For from here the world had blessed peace,
And still the warbler's call
Gives to the weary soul release
Within this forest hall.

I happily lingered in that grove
And loath was I to leave,
For in that place gave thoughts of love
Nor did my spirit grieve.
And as I wandered down that hill
I gentle backwards glanced;
And thought I saw her, happy still
Where all the bluebells danced.

November Leaves

See the November woods now bared
Still speak of leaves yet still to fall,
And naked have the branches shared
With gathered thought full winter's call.

Each glade now fills with deeper piles,
Lo! Hushed and stilled the avenued trees
Have covered up their many aisles
With leaves from many a whispered breeze.

Quiet the leaves have drifting fell
And lighted soft or gently down,
Then riverborne swept through this dell
And spread this glorious autumn gown.

Some final leaves still linger on
To meet the coming wintrous rain,
And flutter above where late have gone
Their fellows, lost to the countried lane.

Borne on the air they raging fly
By winds of change both loud and fierce,
And blown about they final sigh
When last they rest in leafy tiers.

Lines Composed by Brotherswater

So lovely a spot hath God seldom better made;
A ewe is before me on the dew-filled grass,
Her tender lamb beside her in feeding swayed
As this heated hour doth heavy onward pass.
So blessed am I within this sequestered vale
Hail Brotherswater! Thy lasting imagery
Of waters sparkling deep could never fail
To rise impressive. Nor could thy sight be
Aught to my mind but saved perfection.
Nor rocky hillside roundsome steeped with trees
Above these glassy deeps seek out correction.
'Tis so idyllic! A goosander pair now gently sieve
The crystal water as they glide silent by,
Thence to my mind doth nature feeling give
Unto any heart a long and generous sigh.
And here, in this valed seclusion
'Mid all this mountained splendour,
Come thoughts of man and of his late intrusion
With thoughts of farms and sheep intrusive tender.
Thence firmly clear doth mindful in me sail
All of this that our great God downward laid –
To form from out of nought a timeless dale,
Where words of praise in silence alone are weighed.

Philip Lester

A Storm

Where but the sun, but bare an hour ago
Interlaced each tree with all her blazing fire
And brought with her a golden-embered glow
Upon each leaf that warms the heart's desire;
Behold! Now driven full before the gale
The rain now sweeping comes to bear entire
To swift o'er Rydal's pleasant evening scene
Completes her task and bemisted visions sire.

Yet not content with swirling cloud about,
The scene enfolds intense a further hour;
As o'er each crag and peak, a rout
Of increased storm unfolds its mighty power.
And now each tree is equal fearsome tossed,
Each fragile leaf clings desperate in the bower
In desperate hope that they will not be lost
As before the heavy blast they shaken feeble cower.

A blasted tree now split and weather-torn
Unto the earth falls with its branched breaks,
Its aged trunk all mossed and weather-worn
In saddened scene now even further makes.
The deluge persists! The clouded heavens part
As with a wrath renewed, the sombre woodland shakes;
And fresher winds now formed about the start,
Come frenzied forth in gathered wilder wakes.

And now, beside the shelter of a broken wall
A single ewe, her darling lamb now close
'Neath terrored blast and even-tempered squall
Shelters within her sodden-fleeced repose;
Her miseried look betakes her tender plight,
As 'neath the gale in simplest manner chose,
She sets her face and single sight
And calm her charge of all its mounting woes.

Whence, as some mythic Thor in fury and disgrace
Doth raise Mjolnir in his battled cry,
And o'er each wildest place set before his face,
Now angered storms and rages onward by.
'Til exhausted spent his father Odin speaks
Soft to his son in his forgiving sigh
And orders calm, thence furthered ordered seeks
For him to rest and no more his patience try.

Thence peace! The wounded glade now guards
With but a calm, the woodland drops her tears.
And limbs of trees in lost and broken shards
Lie on the ground, like countless fractured spears.
The every leaf as made of polished shield
Upon their surface gathered, now exceeding wears
A fresher mantle in radiance now revealed
As all about the gathered eve, the day now final cheers.

Philip Lester

Composed by Grasmere

Here by an elm I sit, the Lakeland eve now late
Within a bower chosen through its pastoral state;
In observance of nature, who doth never cease
To rest from labours in her changesome lease.
Each humble flower deep hidden in the grass
Breaks from a soiled home in firm intent to pass
From cold to heat, thence labours full to climb
And greet the sun thence live a life sublime.
The insects and the bees busied o'er each fragrant shrub,
Though short a life, do in their vibrance rub
To spread the pollen throughout the verdant earth,
Thence promote each bouqueted bloom of tender worth.
The ash and elm overhead that sprang from seed,
Their boughs entwined now spiralled heavenward lead
With roots that deep fall into the wormy ground,
To eager hold on life with anchors perfect bound.
And blue tits now seek throughout each leafy bower
Regardful of need and of their fervent power;
Their life like candles lit with flaming light
That burn now framed in image twice as bright.
Each heathered place upon the mountain steeps
In slumbrous month now rests, yet later heaps
The gloried hills in all their purpled show.
Each stream that runs from rocky heights
Falls endless down in sparkling clear delight,
Then timeworn meets this deep and ageless lake,
Which speaks a birth of once her glacial break.
And 'neath those cold and glassy deeps
The silvered trout her own appointment keeps;
With lakeborne grebes who also seek to feed

Her tender firstborn, hid within the reed.
Now, rills and eddies form, borne upon the wind
And speak each Lakeland path they are assigned.
Then gently passes the unseen breeze
That stirs both waters and the leaves of trees.
And now, here I too sit, busied upon nature's role
Thence long have pondered on her earthly goal,
Thus observed that quiet she makes a steady course
Desirous full that life succeed in every shape and force.

Helvellyn Viewed

Depart o clouds and let me warm embrace
Helvellyn's peak in all her beautied form,
That doth this vale her presence powering grace
And cause the heart towards her gently warm.

'Tis not that I care not for this present view
Herein I mark that rarer could aught compare;
For once, where glacial masses grew
Is left an excellence well proportioned there.

Lo! I see a glimmer, the mists are lifting clear,
No more her peaks are wrapped in stormy cloud
O come! Give full my heart desirous cheer
Thence dissipate full such unbecoming shroud.

At last! The veiled mists on thee are gone,
And discernible form comes swiftly into view.
No more do visible vapours linger further on,
Nor with obstruct in clouds of vaporous dew.

Helvellyn! Thy waking borders now I full discern
And with what fealty I find upon your sight
As now o'er fairest Thirlmere my heart needs fly
To fill my soul with all your majestic delight.

By a Boathouse on Windermere

The mossy boathouse door full does bear
Witness to infrequent visits to the boat within;
The aged owner and all his household kin
No longer for their age do for it care.
Nor across the meadow late have been
To unlatch eager the firm-placed lock
And once in the craft then lakebound fare.

But how calm and peaceful it is here
As the wind runs the boathouse eaves
And breathes gently o'er the glinting leaves
High above the lake now glassy clear.
Now a sigh all nature generous heaves
Through her bounteous love of life
Upon the place known once as Winandermere.

The pochard and mallard in their rafts
Safe found upon the glassy deep,
Contented drift upon the waters, half asleep
Whilst the wintrous sun in pleasing hafts
Her company does them warming keep.
And after each passing cloud dances
O'er the waters in her beaming shafts.

No more could I wish for than to be
As the grace-filled swan now vivid white
Before me; her colour in the lake mirrored bright
Twofold and double pleasing in imagery.
Such is the creativity of God in sight,
Yet I in wretched sin am tainted locked
All else before me in virtue – free.

A Little Girl with Strawberries

She sat and with delighted thought
A strawberry she placed upon her lips,
And dwelling on the flavour caught
Consumed it gently in little sips.

Her loving eyes reflected smile
That crossed her mind and she did bare
Within a space, so short a while
Her reddened lips in laughter fair.

So carefully pressed she in the dish
Within her gentlest touch;
To soak her last full-berried wish
Within the juice she loved so much.

And then in closing a radiant smile
Come from so little a portioned meal
Came flowing and for a while,
Reigned supreme upon the berried peel!

A Conversation with a Cat

'Tis no pleading with that sorried look
From the glassy window sill.
It was not I but thee who took
The mouse against her will.
Your waiting for her brought reward
Beside her homed retreat,
You caught her life and then you pawed
The victim quite complete!

Nay, 'tis no good using that plaintive cry,
Nor tapping on the pane;
With gentle claw and wondering why
Entry you shall not gain!
I know 'twas natural for you to be
A stalker of your prey,
And nature calling loud in thee
Refused you to say nay.

But nature bides also in my mind,
And I cannot ignore the fact
That to all mercies you were blind
And all compassion lacked!
But Nemesis loveth mice as well
And in me did arouse
A need for justice that on thee fell,
In exile from the house!

By a Farm at Nightfall

A vision I had one autumnal eve
A vision warm and clear,
Of reverie that did perfect leave
An impression held most dear.

A shepherd made his weary way
Across a valley stilled
Where dancing ribbons of sunset play
And larks their dream fulfilled.

Two faithful dogs trotted one each side
With panting breath, their gaze
Looked up alternate to one whose stride
Made for the gloomy haze.

No words could equal such a sight,
Of day's long labour full done;
Or inward measure such delight
As day her course had run.

Immeasurable, the sun's last rays
Played golden as they fell
And slowly measured in unknown ways
Behind the cottaged dell.

The farmer's voice gave no command,
The farmyard gate was breached
As sunlight left the wooded land,
His dogs their kennels reached.

Shadows crept swift upon the farm,
A single light burned bright.
The scene, though sunless spoke of warm
Throughout the darkening night.

Nay, all the stars that shone aloft
Within their heavened space,
Could never equal warmth so soft
That came from such a place.

That single light, unlike the sun,
Whose warmth crept o'er my skin,
Crept in my heart and round it spun,
A joyous flame within.

An Estuary Walk

Where shelduck walk the sanded banks
Between each cockled bed,
And streamlets gleam like little stars
As through the banks they thread;
I walk the barren softened sand
Amongst the plaintive cries
Of gulls that wheel above my head
Beneath cerulean skies.

By aged ship and rotted barge I roam,
Their forms a-hidden deep
Within their embracing sanded home
Embedded fast, they sleep!
Past timbers broken, blackened by age
Where countless tides have raced
Upon them, and twice daily sweep
To cover their rotted waste.

Across the wide expanse of sand
And onwards to the sea,
With ne'er a soul to view at hand
Or speak in company;
I walk where tiny moistened heaps
Lie spiral in their mounds,
And gentle thoughts speak soft to me
Of worms upon their rounds.

Behind me now those black ribbed shapes
Lie almost hid from view,
And on I walk where the river drapes
O'er sands of changesome hue;
Across the bar where curlews rise
And voice their warning sound,
Where ducks have gathered, no little few
Upon the tidal ground.

O what peace there is within this place
To hear the lonesome cries;
To stand and but for a time erase
All of life's false lies.
To hear the surf and gulls in cry,
To view the tide-filled sea,
To dream of loves that never die,
And glimpse eternity.

P L

Philip Lester

A New Bridge Taken by a Flood

Who would have thought that use of thee
Would last so short a time?
Yet, denied in full in that passage free,
From field to wooded climb.
The ash that once for years fourscore
Adorned this rivered place
Hath fallen ever and will no more
Her roots now earthward chase.

For eaten away is the soil that bound
That gloried ash in leaf,
And left is nought but a soiled mound
To this, the rivered thief.
The boundless force of rain in force
Hath caused a mighty flood
And robbed a beauty of its source
From out the aged wood.

Free passage thence! The tree outcried
Before all wood and stone;
Yet passage was to her denied
And thence in flood was thrown.
Both watered might and rooted tree
Against the pillared bed,
Yet stone held firm and easily
'Gainst nature firmly led.

Whereon in anger further weighed
Her wrath was treeborne said,
And nature uneager to be held or swayed
Took half the bridge, instead!

Ode to the River Swale

O how could I a riverside wanderer fail
To love such passioned moods
As rise possessive in your name?
O see! The trout who 'neath thy surface broods
Hath rose and kissed thee in gentlest hail.
And late by thee since first I happy came,
Each mayfly hath danced with joy about
Thence on your waters lighted.
The Dipper too, who slight above thine embrace
Now eager flits upstream and down
In joyous feeling, nor is content
To o'er waters roam but gathers 'neath your crown
Whatso'er insect life may tinied race,
'Twixt every stone and niche that you have sent
To promote his life so tender,
And there content he feeds, delighted.
But what of your changesome moods, o river?
Ye have so many! From the crystal eddied pool
Deep formed yet clear to the pebbled bed below,
To other waters dark and deep and cool,
O thou abundant giver!
And of tempestuous floods, where once a boy did go
No more to return to his mother's arms
Whose love ye ever blighted.

Yet who could blame these waters that wind
Through valley deep with woods that speak a grace.
An innocence found, a beauty that the eye
May with its gleaning mindward inward trace.

'Tis such a marvel to our earthly mind
That oft in our hearts is heard the gentlest sigh,
For this is perfection that we see, no more,
That from God's hands to us at first alighted.

From St. Bees Cliffs

I look back from my sought-for promontory
And lo! St Bees lies before me nestled
In her harbour, snug as a throstle in her nest.
O but 'tis such a wondrous day! Blue skies
Were never bluer, the clouds gleaming white
Against the clear heavens.
And such a gentle breeze is blowing to dismiss
The heady heat of the day before me.
Nor could it seemingly be better planned,
For now the roar of breaking surf on the shore
Far beneath me resounds full in echoes
As if each wave had a voice of its own;
Whilst about me kittiwake and fulmar sound
Upon the air a thousandfold.
The horizon is perfect clear and on the waves
A lone fishing vessel moves lazily o'er the scene,
Followed eager by flocks of gulls behind
Yearning for lost fish from nets outflung;
And as I watch all beauty rolls in one thought:
How good it is to be alive this day.

By Lindisfarne Priory

A sadness touches me whilst here I stand
And a sense of loss seems gathered here.
For once, where gathered monks in happy band
Did first this site with hardy mattock tear
The earth and by patient labour,
Commence to build each adjacent neighbour
This priory commissioned by Edward's hand.
See now! For all their effort human wrought
To build of such a marvellous place,
(and they laboured not in vain, yet fought
To serve God well and dwell within His grace).
Is now, nine centuries past or more
But walls that rise from off a grassy base,
And windowed places and pillared tiers
With doors that too have also even ceased
And decay, that forever endless rears
Its head o'er nave and chancel west to east.
Yet another theme speaks soft to sadness felt
As sun sinks down and into the sea doth melt,
That gladdens my heart and in prospect cheers.
For sequestered here I saw not a priory
Ruined, but where the great architect passing by
Had chosen out for altar the endless sea
And for this roofed church the endless vaulted sky.

Cairngorm Summit in midwinter

When first ascends some man to steady climb
To mountain summit gripped in ice and snow,
Thence met by winds across the hoary rime
That sudden doth fierce and angered on him blow,
He cannot help but feel a smallness found
Against some great giant that before him lies,
As all about him white majesty is wound,
And snow about him gentle whirls and flies!

Yet oft, as some David before the Philistine
Who regarded as nought the giant in his size,
But simple took a pebble rounded fine
And let fly the blow betwixt his haughty eyes,
May man too by simple steady toil the same
With ice axe up the windward place be sent;
And smite the head from off the giant's frame
Thence place a treasure into his memoried tent.

Falls of Bruar

Old place of pilgrimage I have been
Unto your pine-filled banks,
And with a gladsome eye have seen
Deep wooded pines in ranks.
Each winding place, thy natured arch
With waters that generous flow,
A hundred feet near wher'er the larch
Else fir straight laced grow.

Lo! The ravine speaks out an icy birth
O'er boulders vast ancient strewn,
And speaks a time of an icy girth
And ten thousand winters hewn.
Yet to the bridge, high o'er this gorge,
I revel about the span,
That bridges the chasm God once made
To merge full with the world of man.

By a Canalside

I recent passed by the age-old canal,
And where once stood the creaking timbered lock
That I recall as a wandering child
The waters now stood in different obedience;
Not held back by the unique craft of the joiner,
But by invention that spewed forth concrete
And set forth in scanty hours' work
A cold barrier against the lapping waters.
Making the laboured stroke of chisel
And plane and saw a mockery.
Thence I looked to the silent water beyond;
Waters that once upheld each noble barge,
Barges that for ages plied their craft
'Twixt towns and cities in their trade.
The jovial bargee aboard with his fellow,
The gleaming paint of the vessel;
Borne bright and decorative painted.
Thence aboard, the coal, the iron, the wood
Stowed in daily round of industry,
And the immense Clydesdale before it,
Pulling with seeming ease the craft behind.
The buckler, the hammers, the taut rope
With legs of power that moved trade onward.
Thence that marvellous vision changed,
And blackish waters came, chemically invaded;
Steam pipes overhead, weeded overgrown places,

Bicycles, perambulators, bottles thrown careless
Into the waters, secreted not from the eye.
Discard from the uncaring in an uncivilised world.
Whilst about it, in this decadent scene,
A lone moorhen threaded her way onward,
Leading her tender brood amid the wreckage
As a small candle, lit to light this
Darkened room about it.

In the Depths of Redesdale

So silent and stilled is the air
About me now as I onward walk.
So lovely is this peace, so fair
That loath am I even to whisperous talk.
The very sweetness of these pines
Upon each heavy bough reclines,
'Neath the weight of summer's care
As the sun o'erpowering shines.

Thence onward through the forest deep
In silence, save broken by the sound
Of my footsteps echoing 'neath pines that weep
Their dews to the needled ground.
Else voiced this whose sweetest call
Pervades the depths of some nearby aisles,
Thence, carried up each pined hall,
I journey on for hours and miles.
Yet as I have through forest paced,
Strange whispers have I heard;
As if each tree had breathed in haste
Some swiftly passing word.
And now the forest path hath led
Past final the trees at last,
Yet surely a pine could not have whisperous said,
'Twas an axeless human passed!

Gordale Scar

No glacial mass is found here any more,
Or rivers that rage, but now the gentlest stream
Doth from the heights cascading ever pour,
In sunlight soft and flowing gentle gleam.
Yet seek o friend and cast a searching eye
To evidenced views across the limestone scar,
And to the past let forth imagined fly
O'er scenes depictive and now distant far.

To vallied sides, now steep and smooth in grass,
Where perchance a glacier else a rivered course
Came through this hallway and did even pass
With all its great and overwhelming force.
Else, o'er the years did through a cavern race
Some ice or power that journeyed on its way
Until the roof cried out ''tis done'
And collapsed then to the rivered place.

Thence, having scoured out wide and deep
The barren land, the ice begins retreat,
And waters gentler then begin to leap
Else o'er the caved remains less harsher beat.
Yet halls about still echo of the past
Throughout a gorge that speaks impressive still,
As through the bygone cave, a waterous blast
Doth roar in splendour 'neath the craggy hill.

Philip Lester

The Ruined Fountain Remembered Whole

Was it not here, when I a mere boy of ten
Did cease from play and panting rest?
And accompanied by others of my age and ken
Stood eager by thee? And was blessed
With refreshing waters that forceful broke
In fountained fashion by passing folk
Yet more for child than use of men?

And how we laughed by your stone surround,
When one of us would take his eager turn
And as one drank, with ne'er an uttered sound
We crept to where the tap beneath the urn
Lay waiting for us to press but harder still
And shower the thirsting visitor 'til
With hastened retreat, the moment there was crowned!

O where is the use in thee my friend of now?
Thy bowl has rusted and lost its silver gleam,
Thy tap has broken, I see not ever how
Shall come again that once clear silver stream,
That came so joyful to my boyish lips –
And flowed so clean in all those wanton sips.
Alas! Gone is that youth and gone o friend art thou!

Upon the Stern Deck of a Ship

Motion! The endless motion of a tireless sea,
Constant changing her face of grey and green.
Lo! The waves rolling forth to greet the eye.
And the breeze! A gentle breeze blowing
That stirs the air so gently in movement unseen.
Now behind us a whitened gannet hugging
Close the ocean crest in hunger,
Thence high up in the air, thence downward plunging
Into the restless waters beneath him.
And the wake! Behind us the great wake of the ship
Spreading wide and clear, proclaiming loud
Our passage homeward.
Thence in other whiteness now, the ethereal spirit
Of a kittiwake rises, white on white to observe
Our laboured passage onward.
Now nightfall! Each star lit above,
Cast deep into the wondrous night-time sky,
And the restful lulling motion of the ship,
Whilst occasioned distant vague shapes of vessels
Journeying elsewhere with onboard lights of greeting
To us, paled and dim beneath the beautied stars above.

Beside the River Brathay

What drew me to this rivered place,
Where ripples rise soft from off its face?
And hoverflies drinking from some nectared head
Of scabeous stems beside the river bed
In seeming visioned grace.
The shallowed pools here all bedecked
With fern and grassy stems erect,
And occasioned harebells softly sprayed
With moistured drops from the river weighed,
Whose journey swift hath flecked.

And how soft she glides, to where – God knows!
As peace within my mind now flows.
And a dipper passing takes full his leave,
As under the bridge 'twixt banks doth weave
Where kingcup and bistort grows.
Thou mother! O lull me upon thy breast
With sounds harmonious from off thy crest,
With lights that soft and sparkling crown
And glinting shards that roll ever down,
Murmur soft, I sink to rest.

Philip Lester

Lines Composed in a School Classroom

O give me I pray those times again,
Far, far removed from the world of men.
Who know not how to live in peace
And who seem to argue without cease,
O'er matters fully beyond their ken
With tongues of unbridled lease.

Now each man to my life it seems
Forced to fulfil his selfish dreams,
And each one now knows best o'er all –
Yea! Now within each the teacher doth call,
But now here, now firm wisdom seems
Nor seeming calls to all.

Nay, but give to me that classroom small,
With innocent pictures upon the wall
Of animals drawn with loving care,
(though obscure somewhat to adult stare)
Of rhymes and tables that I recall,
Above some teacher's chair.

O where has that love now fleeting sailed,
That once I saw when the child prevailed?
No colour different of persons then,
No hatred, nor malice, nor even when
Those heady classroom lessons failed
Did we become as heartless men.

My life then was governed and there did rise
A wisdom before my tender eyes,
And teachers came governed by the Queen,
Hence further to this I welcome glean,
That far above her and above the skies
God ruled all things unseen.

O I would gladly have those days again,
Those days of joy and gain;
When childish praises sounded clear
To drown each foreboding worldly fear,
When Jesus alone did reign.

The thought of Him in righteous rule,
With heaven's wisdom o'er each school,
And governing thence from childish plan,
From infancy to life's full span
(Whose wisdom maketh man the fool)
Has dawned for child – why not for man?

Philip Lester

When Unseen Angels Pass

Do trees bend boughs when'er they pass
Above their verdant leaves?
Or ice floes break to shard-formed glass
Amid those ice strewn seas?
Or mountains spew their lava forth
And reddened march en masse?
Or fires rage fierce from south to north,
Sped by their wing-borne breeze!

Nay! When angels espy the created earth,
Their passing (though unseen)
Is there in pureness at each birth
Where God their joy hath been.
And where a quiet place is found
There one hath taken rest –
Nor are they met but once in sound
But quiet watch, serene.

O'er all creation swift they fly
O'er time which they ignore,
And o'er each repentant sinner cry
As if joy could rise no more.
The babe who in her fragile cote
Sees them as through a glass,
And giddy laughter there is wrote
When unseen angels pass.

A Horse in Desperation

Poor creatures! A premonition mild
Had I that something would go amiss.
For as your rider (no more than a child)
Walked on before me, I sensed that this
Felt more than met the casual eye.

Then the petulant lip upon her moved
And as if to promote her anger as she walked,
And of thee she loudly disapproved,
Thence to thee passionate talked
Of misbehaviour and of her unseating.

But no more could she climb back
Upon thy dark and handsome frame,
For doubtless of skill she had great lack
In horsemanship, but to thee apportioned blame
Thence raised her fearsome crop.

Once, twice, thrice upon some tender flank
She laid there unjust blows,
Whilst all the while towards the bank
(Where water liquid flows)
You moved to avoid her temper fierce.

Philip Lester

Thence I lost sight of thee and her both,
But for times briefest space
For deep in converse with another, I was loath
To after thee firm race
And give to that child my piece of mind.

But here now you bide in waters cold,
The passer-by has caught hold of the rein,
So that your head he might but hold;
And by the end of your flowing mane
The melted ice floe floats.

And there she sits, the equestrian maid,
Sobbing well for sympathy;
The innocent now, but one who flayed
A gentle creature not moments by,
Thence drove it frantic from her whip.

But now, with sufficient force gathered,
We have at last secured a hold.
Lo! Now with all your muzzle lathered
And freezing body, filled with cold,
We thence raise thee from the ice.

No matter this her fault, nor is it said
But asked of it, she mentions not her crop
Thence says 'he but himself had led
Himself to slip' for thence she saw him drop!
Poor creature! If he could but talk!

Hence, let us hope it teaches well the child
To take more heed for anger less,
To relate the truth and be affirmed mild,
To hold herself in more gentleness –
And refrain from horses!

Philip Lester

The Child in a Nighttime Wood

I recall when I was once a child
Scarce fifteen summer past,
From out the house one summer evening mild
To the woods mine eye I cast.
And there, the forest my heart beguiled
Thence to her bowers I passed.
Such narrow aisles I peaceful viewed
Upon that rarest eve.
A place where oft the buzzard did weave,
And where countless pine and larch were queued
I watched the sunset leave.
Such quiet was upon that place,
Such calm that scarce a sound
Proceeded from that interlace
As dusk her mantle wound.
And darkly there the dusk did erase
Each tree and path and ground.
Each bough then dipped in red or brown
Or fiery hues of gold,
Gave farewell as the sun sank down
And embers then turned cold.
Then soft the night did all things crown
As darkness did unfold.
Then did I no more find delight
Nor beauty in that glade.
My heart (but then unused to night)
Forsook that sheltered shade;
And eager for comfortous light

My footsteps I lengthy made.
Then looked I to all shapes about
Which danced, and grey I saw
Deceptive shadows that gave doubt
As fear upon me wore.
And from my steps a steady rout
Within me thence did pour.
I walked and cantered, then I paced
To quit that shadowed fear,
And as each shade upon me raced
My own footsteps did I hear,
Thence in my heart was fearful placed
The thought of spectres near!
Each leaf beneath my footsteps' fall
Caused more of doubt within,
And throughout that leafy narrow hall
My braveness shrank to thin
(As round about each forest wall
Seemed thence to narrow in!)
I ran! Then as my legs firm strode
My breathing grew afire,
As down that path my limbs full flowed
Until a fenced wire
Broke to my sight, and all of that abode
Sank swift in firm retire.
Thence I looked back on the fading sight
Of that forest far and near,
Where risen moon gave off her light
Through skies of brightness clear,
Thence pondered full on foolish flight
And how beauty could cause such fear.

Philip Lester

On Summer's Wealth

I heard a cuckoo calling clear the morn
In early rising at the gates of dawn,
Bade summer enter! And ere upon each field
Where settled wall or hedge was sealed
In liquid approval gave out his happy sound,
And o'er the lambs and sheep did resound
A blessing to each ear! Thence shadows fell,
The busied farmer his dog obedience tell,
As before the aged and rusted iron gate
He crouched impassive, his master's voice to wait.
Thence a warbling thrush gave voiced sound
From out a heady rowan in claimed abode,
With liquid music from out his breast
In proud design of dam upon her nest
Of blush eggs – each pastelled heady hue
Now fills the mind with vision of hazed blue.
And from a peaceful arbour drone the bees,
Busied thus, midst flower, shrub and trees.
And lo! Here I sit, like to Jonah stayed
'Neath a gourded tree bequeathed in happy shade.
Each birdsong competes with vibrant thrush,
The visiting warbler in his haven lush
Doth call; the robin far or blackbird near
In passioned mood rejoices loud and clear.
And in the heat-filled distant dim, a raven in a niche
Of rocky knoll and shade doth rested reach,
From summer's heat; each creature now hath chose
To hide from heat in forced repose.
The chorused birds and each mountain round about

All in glory speaks with ne'er a doubt.
For there states a theme for all the world to see –
That the best things in life are truly given free.

Lines Composed on a Trip Around Isle Martin

Dip o little craft, gentle dip!
And o'er each new wave peaceful slip.
To master each swell is thus thy right.
Come! Another ripple now gives thee flight.
O how motioned now the prow doth grip
The formed ocean bright!

Come closer isle, I long to see
Each wave as firm she breaks on thee;
Beneath the home where the Guillemot
Hath chose her narrow-ledged nesting spot,
To lay her egg in firmest safety
Upon her stony cot.

Our boat is song and welcome sings!
The sea is kind, she gives us wings,
As by each seal's enquiring gaze
We pass in hail, and saluting raise
Each emergent head that clings
To each new tidal phase.

Slow round Isle Martin we press,
Whose seaweed coves darkest impress;
Where cormorant bask on their rocky seat,
And fulmar in their glidesome beat
Pass bold above the ocean crest
With wings outstretched and neat.

Lo! O'er each deep we questing rove
By craggy cliff and seaswept cove.
And to each new sight we firm approve,
As slow past each new buttress we move.
Thence hail each gull fixed hung above
Within an endless vaulted roof.

P.L.

A Lost Path

O Friend, the path that once we found
Some score of years now past
Eludes me still; I memoried cast
Our times then together, then round and round
The chambers of my mind is no more
That summer path we found upon our tour.

'Twas a day like this of rain and sun
When to this village we did repair,
And in the height of youth, our care
Seemed scarcely had begun;
As round these streets our converse did sound
Its presence and our footsteps firm resound.

The lake still is as it was before
The fields I exact recall;
And where the mountains gently fall
My memory refreshes more.
And still the church has chiming power
Above the woodland bower.

Yet faded is that favoured place
Where once our youth gave rise
Where birelessly we seemed to race
'Neath endless summered skies.

On Seeing a Shooting Star

Look! To the east a radiant show
Against the sacred night
Doth burn the sky with perfect glow
Within her trailing flight,
And close behind her tresses show
In myriad delight.

Whence came thee? From some far-off place
A million miles but past?
Lo! I see thee o'er our heavens race
In final triumphed blast.
I see thee gleam, thy fiery pace
As final here now cast.

Farewell! Thou starry messenger fell,
The last of thee hath died,
But what message didst thou brief foretell
Across the heavens wide?
Was it ill or was it well?
The question in me doth bide.

Philip Lester

Upon a Scottish Mountain

One glorious April morn I left the quiet road
Where Loch Tay's tribute waters gentle flowed.
And stepping forth amid the lichened pine,
I drank in that Scottish air like fragrant wine.
Slow laboured I upon those grassy heights,
By glacial rock that lay at rest from flight;
O'er grassy bank withered both by ice and sun,
To where the view my heart at once had won.
And lo! The scene unfolded thus before my eyes,
I saw as when the eagle up high soaring flies;
Beneath me all lay visioned in a glance,
And my eyes from vale to mount did happily dance.
And thoughts aspired within my beating breast,
That there I sat where none before had taken rest.
O, the air lay still about me and quite serene;
Blue skies adorned full that mountain scene.
To the northwest snow lay on Ben Nevis' mount
Whilst eastward Ben Lawers did in like account
Rise impressive up to meet each passing cloud;
Her sharpened peaks immersed in hazy shroud.
And long I sat on Ben More's ageless braes
And restful on those heights I loving gazed –
To where Stob Binnein's perilous face did fall
And thus with quietude, I did at length forestall
No longer the need to take in that distant view,
But passed slow upward to heights anew.
'Twas a joy to walk upon that highland peak,
Snow lay dispersed and warm rays did seek
The corniced icefields, which did barely last
In quiet remind of last winter, final passed.

I came by way of Stob Coire, and in ascent
Passed where Meall Na Dige did firm relent.
Her rolling hillsides bore my footsteps down
To where the valley in her lush spring gown
Rolled gentle and sure towards the forest glade.
And there amongst the pines I found the shade
Refreshing cool against my heated face,
As along the track I joyful homeward raced.

P.L

Philip Lester

Upon the Moor (a fragment)

Upon the moor, upon the moor
Upon the wild, wild moor.
Where curlew fly and grouse alarmed rise
I bide happy 'til day is o'er.
And all day long I have rest where lies
My heart by heaven's door.

Lo! So sombre a place there never was
Where colours all have waned,
And where each well-hid channel formed
Where countless years have rained,
The acid peat hath canker stormed
And through each passage drained.

But I care not whether sun or rain
Before me here hath been,
For cloud may roll or sunshine cast
Upon each moorland scene.
For well I know in each moment passed
Framed wilderness shall I glean!

Owen the Rock

Owen Jasper has a Welsh farmer been
These seventy years and more,
Yet still is he a-shearing seen
With sheep about five score.
Then off he goes each summer's eve
For his twice cup of tea and a slice
Of breaded jam, which he will never leave
Nor his brew at anyone's price.
And Owen says, 'wife, please further may I
Have a slice more of jam wi' some bread?'
But Owen's wife each time will deny
The request that Owen has said.
Then it's off down the road to shearing again
For two or three hours of more sheep;
His labours continue, two score in the pen
Before Owen goes homeward to sleep.
And he smiles as he shears (and often he sings)
Whilst working all day with the flock,
For oft in his mind, in proudness still rings
His nickname – Owen the Rock.

Upon the Return of Halley's Comet

How long-lived thou art, o starry messenger,
Trailing o'er the centuries past
Your arrivals seen in regular time.
O how immense the trail of thee is cast
Throughout creation's rhyme.
By Orion, thence on to Aldebaran,
Past the cluster of Pleiades,
Thy lengthy journey of endless span
Doth flow with seeming ease.
And I marvel thus that on this spot
Where upon my foot hath stood
That man's aged years by seventied lot
Is taken oft-times by the flood
Of time and aged works fulfilled
Upon his feeble frame.
And yet out there, thou art not stilled
But continue on in name;
And the glory of thee wanders still
Throughout each far-told place,
Whilst here, the furtherance of God's will
Binds man to meet His grace.

The Blue tit in the Apple Tree

See! See! 'tis a joy to watch thee on the bough
When full in searching with your eye,
The daintiest morsel you once allow
Within your mouth as you pass by.

See! See! Amid the blossom you gently peep,
With fluttering wings your form hangs free;
Then upside down I see you creep
A-searching then inquisitively.

See! See! Another form like thine appears
Searching like thee, 'tis my belief;
Lo! How your agility warming cheers
In scrutiny of every leaf.

See! See! How quickly now the branches there
Have been inspected in searching glance;
How swiftly your moves in patient care
Portrays your warm and sprightly dance.

See! See! How little now the branch hath stirred
Within your leaving flight.
Thou gentle sight, thou sprightly bird
How well you give delight!

Notre Dame

Behold! I see your blessed spires,
And sweet from out your temple's aisles
Come faithful voices in rejoice,
Then out the mouths of reverent choirs,
The echoed sound of choral hymn
To each heart warms and gentle fires.

Those echoed voices lift in sound,
Their praises sung in hymned verse;
And forth unto each blessed place,
Wher'er each niche is holy crowned
(Or holds the centuried hallowed seal)
Comes praise and love from hearts profound.

Lo! Deep within your masoned bowers,
Your windows steep in glorious tale
Of holy scribe and honoured saint
Which all the passing light empowers,
Are held in place like precious jewels
Which well the reverent heart devours.

Upon these pillars with wondrous gaze
And upward with a searching eye,
I marvel that the thoughts of men
Should such a shrine to God thus raise;
Within the aisles of Notre Dame
A temple fitting, filled with praise.

Ye parapets that always silent speak
Of revolution seen before your stone;
What stories could your walkways tell
Of historic import; and right well unique
Of conflict borne within your streets,
Beneath each brassed and reverential peak.

How oft your bells have rung out loud,
And as a voice each door well hails
To each, as far as sound thus permits
O'er each new dawn (through right or wrong).
To each from off this Parisian isle
Call one and all to mass and holy song!

Untouched she stands! Serene by every age,
Whilst all about a regular decay
Has flown throughout each measured street;
And to the eye the centuries in their rage
Have left to her a beauty undenied; yet man
About her beautied sight, oblivious, seeks his wage.

Upon a Yorkshire Fell

I have sat atop this grassy knoll 'twixt one vale and another
And thought on thee in quietude, dear friend and brother.
On how we two have on countless occasions past
Some similar view had, our single gazing cast
To creation from off our verdant earthy seat,
Ere sat restful 'neath gentle winds on days of summer's heat.

Thence I thought on our friendship long and how that harmony
Came thus to blend, complete it seemed, with all that I did see.
As if the all were meant to be a single measure
And spake a love, a fealty that was to God a pleasure.
Yet sad it is that such a view from off a grassy cote
Is nought to some with visioned gift, for blindness oft is wrote.
And sad I am for an aching world through famine or the sword
Thence sad for the life where a friend such as thee
Or a view such as this hath not poured.

Owl by Night

In dead of night, his eye a-bright,
Where collects the piney dew,
There sits secreted from all sight
A shape of darkish hue;
Within the fur, without a stir,
With ears of deep intent;
He descries the move of mousy fur
And drinks the blooded scent.

Then winged he sweeps and frozen leaps
The prey to rigid stance;
And out before his talon reaps
The victimed final dance.
A cry ascends, he full descends,
The life is cast aside.
And blooded prey he quiet rends
While young the night doth bide.

Philip Lester

Philip Lester

Philip Lester was inspired as a youth with the Lakeland Poets, a passion for nature and art and in addition to writing poetry is an accomplished self-taught artist with exhibitions throughout the country. He lives in Brampton with a vast collection of Doctor Who paraphernalia and a rescue dog called Faith who rules the household.

Lightning Source UK Ltd.
Milton Keynes UK
UKHW012114260821
389499UK00001B/35